W9-BOB-680

"THE PHILLIES AND
PHILADELPHIA
WILL FOREVER
HOLD A VERY
SPECIAL PLACE
IN MY HEART."

—Mike Schmidt

101 Reasons to Love the
PHILLIES

Ron Green, Jr.

Stewart, Tabori & Chang
New York

Introduction

For generations, fans of the Philadelphia Phillies have kept the faith, despite the seemingly perpetual disappointment their baseball team delivered. Phillies fans have been many things—coarse, hoarse, and unforgiving come quickly to mind—but they've never been spoiled by success. They've never had the chance.

But they've always had the faith, no matter how hard they tried to hide it.

Charles McGlone, a genuine son of Philadelphia, claimed not to care for the Phillies. For decades, they would tease him in springtime, torture his summers, and then, mercifully, die like the leaves in the fall.

He said he didn't care whether they won or lost, claimed he wouldn't watch them, and yet every time his son, John, would call, Charles could rattle off every little detail about what the Phillies were—or weren't—doing.

There's something about baseball that reaches beyond the standings and statistics. Particularly in a place like Philadelphia, where the Phillies have spanned three centuries, there's a tie that binds not just fans to the team but families to one another. For Phillies fans, it means remembering the Baker Bowl, the City Series, and Grover Cleveland Alexander. It means the Whiz Kids, Shibe Park, and the Vet. It's Chuck Klein, spring training in Clearwater, Florida, and, yes, even the 23-game losing streak in 1961. It's about the curse of Billy Penn, Jim Bunning's perfect game, and Dick Sisler's home run. It's about all of that and more.

Charles McGlone is gone now but his wife, Irma, still watches the Phillies, visiting Citizens Bank Park on occasion.

And in Charlotte, North Carolina, the McGlone family—John; his wife, Edie; daughter, Maddie; and son, Jake—spend their springs and summers and falls following the Phillies. It's not just a day-to-day thing but, often, it's inning by inning, at bat by at bat.

The kids have heard about Richie Ashburn and Steve Carlton and Mike Schmidt. Now they have their own heroes, named Ryan Howard, Chase Utley, Jimmy Rollins, and Cole Hamels. In the evenings, they watch the Phillies and keep the faith.

It runs in the family. It runs in thousands of other families around Philadelphia and beyond—a tie that binds.

On October 29, 2008, when the faith was rewarded with the Phillies' second world championship, theirs were the voices we heard. And if you listen closely, you can probably hear them now. Music to Philadelphia ears.

"ALL IS FORGIVEN"

—John McGlone

1 10,000 Losses

It's a perverse point of pride among Phillies fans—being the first and, so far, only major-league team to lose 10,000 games—but it's part of what has made the franchise beloved by so many. Of the 16 original American and National League franchises, Philadelphia was the last to win its first World Series, in 1980.

Ryan Howard during the Phillies'
10,000th loss, July 15, 2007

1884 Phillies

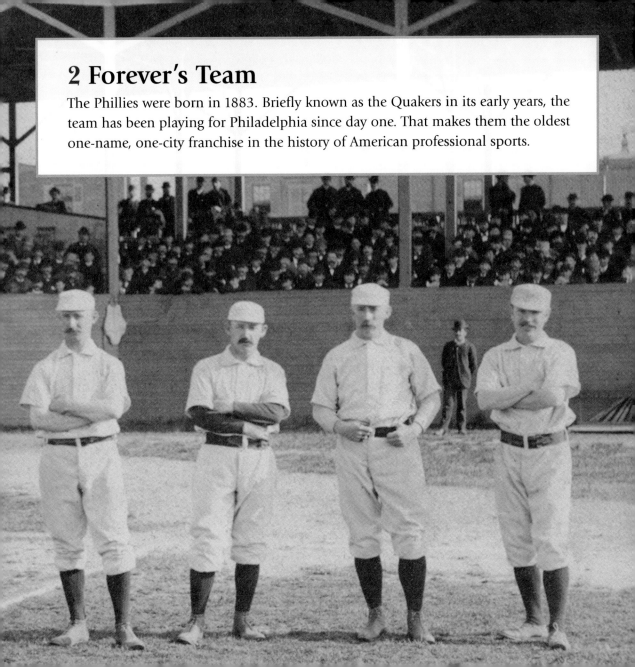

2 Forever's Team

The Phillies were born in 1883. Briefly known as the Quakers in its early years, the team has been playing for Philadelphia since day one. That makes them the oldest one-name, one-city franchise in the history of American professional sports.

3 Baker Bowl

It is nothing but a memory now. No lasting legacy marks its place in history, but Recreation Park was home to the Phillies for four seasons, ending in 1886. Their new home had other official names—the Philadelphia Baseball Grounds and National League Park—but the locals knew the Phillies' home as the Baker Bowl. For nearly 52 seasons the Phillies played there, though without much success, winning just one pennant in that time. It was a park that was regarded as the best in the land when it opened in 1887, though its playing dimensions were considered small even then. Fire destroyed the Baker Bowl in 1894 but the park was fully rebuilt, only to gradually lose its charm. Its most notable feature was its right-field wall, which was located only about 280 feet from home plate (right-center measured 300 feet). To offset the short field, the wall reached 60 feet in the air including the screen topping.

Fans in the right-field bleachers,
Baker Bowl, 1915

Charlie Ferguson

4 Al Reach

He was the first owner of the Phillies, co-founding the franchise after his playing career ended. Reach was more than just a player and owner. He was a major figure beyond the game, speaking on behalf of baseball and later building a sporting-goods business that made him a wealthy man. In 1889, Reach sold his business to Albert Spalding.

5 Charlie Ferguson

Ferguson came to a sad and early end—he died of typhoid fever in 1888 at the age of 25—but his short baseball career was spectacular. In a four-year span, Ferguson was the Phillies' dominant pitcher, winning 99 games. Included was the first no-hitter in Phillies history—a 1–0 win over the Providence Grays—which Ferguson tossed in 1885. Ferguson also led the team with 85 runs batted in and hit .337 in 1887, proving his value as an all-around player. He was so revered that during the first season after his death, several teams wore black on one sleeve to commemorate him.

6 The Left-Handed Catcher

Theories abound about why left-handers don't catch—take your pick. There have been very few of them in the history of major-league baseball. But Jack Clements, who spent most of his 19th-century career with the Phillies, may have been the best. Also a solid power hitter, Clements is the only lefty to catch more than 1,000 games, and he is credited with being the first catcher to wear a chest protector.

"HE WAS THE GAME'S BEST ALL-AROUND PLAYER."

—Bill Hanna on Charlie Ferguson, *Baseball Magazine*, 1924

7 Quakers and Blue Jays

They weren't always known as the Phillies. It just seems that way. In the team's first year of existence, it was known as the Quakers, a nod to the heritage of many of Philadelphia's citizens. By the team's second year, fans had begun calling them the Phillies, and by 1890, Quakers was dropped completely.

GRAHAM-PHILA:NAT.

The years passed and, beginning in 1943, there were a few years when the team had two official names—the Phillies and the Blue Jays. Maybe it was the history of failure, maybe it was boredom, maybe it was a much too early attempt to steal Toronto's thunder. Regardless, proving that not every marketing idea is a good one, the Blue Jays name quietly faded away, much like a few too many Phillies seasons.

8 The Names

Boom-Boom Beck, Rabbit Benton, Sheriff Blake, Cupid Childs, Choo Choo Coleman, Gavvy Cravath, Kiddo Davis, Pickles Dillhoefer, Kid Elberfeld, Rags Faircloth, Peaches Graham, Chicken Hawks, Nippy Jones, Bevo LeBourveau, Peanuts Lowrey, Pinky May, Cyclone Miller, Moon Mullen, Greasy Neale, The Only Nolan, Phenomenal Smith, Cannonball Titcomb, Turkey Tyson, Piggy Ward, and of course, Nap Lajoie, Eppa Rixey, and Billy Sunday.

9 Mighty Casey

Dan Casey, a largely forgettable pitcher for the Phillies in the 1880s, didn't do anything to warrant legendary status, but Casey claimed it anyway. Casey believed himself to be the inspiration for Ernest Lawrence Thayer's famous poem, "Casey at the Bat," though the author never said that. Casey based his assertion on the day he struck out against the New York Giants in 1887, a year before the poem was published. A few days earlier, Casey had hit his only home run of the season, breaking open a tight game, and when he stepped to the plate with the Phillies trailing New York 4–3, two men on, and two outs in the ninth, the notion of another heroic moment came to mind. Naturally, Casey struck out. But his story lives on.

CASEY, PITCHER, PHILA.

"OH, SOMEWHERE IN THIS FAVORED LAND THE SUN IS SHINING BRIGHT; THE BAND IS PLAYING SOMEWHERE, AND SOMEWHERE HEARTS ARE LIGHT, AND SOMEWHERE MEN ARE LAUGHING, AND SOMEWHERE CHILDREN SHOUT; BUT THERE IS NO JOY IN MUDVILLE — MIGHTY CASEY HAS STRUCK OUT."

—Ernest Lawrence Thayer, "Casey at the Bat"

"MORE MEN FAIL THROUGH
LACK OF PURPOSE THAN
LACK OF TALENT."

—Billy Sunday

10 Billy Sunday

Before he became a famous evangelist, Sunday played baseball, and he spent his last days in the game wearing a Phillies uniform. In 1890, his Pittsburgh team was decimated when players left to join a rival league. Sunday was sold to the Phillies in August with the idea that he could help the team win the National League pennant. The Phillies failed to capture the title, however, and Sunday's baseball career came to an end. With a calling to religion, Sunday used his baseball celebrity to help attract crowds when he spoke across the Midwest. As the years went on, Sunday received far more acclaim as a religious figure than he ever did as a baseball player.

Ed Delahanty

11 Ed Delahanty

He played more than a century ago, but Delahanty's achievements still glow. Delahanty hit .400 or better three times in his Hall of Fame career, including a National League–best .410 in 1899. His career batting average of .346 remains among the highest in history. Pehaps the best year of Delahanty's 16-year career came in 1896, when he hit four home runs in one game—all of them inside-the-park homers, making him the only player ever to do that.

12 Sliding Billy Hamilton

There haven't been many like this Phillies Hall of Fame center fielder, who played for the team from 1890 through 1895. Hamilton was a career .344 hitter (he also played for the Kansas City Cowboys and Boston Beaneaters), but his legend was made with his legs. Renowned for the jump he could get leaving first base, Hamilton is one of only three players in history to score more runs (1,691) than the number of games he played in his career (1,578). Hamilton scored 192 runs in 1894, still a single-season record, and his 115 stolen bases in 1891 was the National League record for 80 years.

13 The Hall of Fame Outfield

More than 30 years before the New York Yankees' Murderers' Row became a part of baseball legend, the Phillies had their own collection of Cooperstown-worthy talent, lined up side by side in the outfield. The trio consisted of Ed Delahanty, Billy Hamilton, and Sam Thompson, each of whom has a plaque in the Baseball Hall of Fame. The three played together from 1891 through 1895, and each hit better than .400 in 1894: Hamilton hit .404, and Delahanty and Thompson each hit .407.

Nap Lajoie as a member of
the Philadelphia Athletics

14 The American League Invasion

The Phillies' world was rocked in 1901 when the Athletics—a crosstown franchise and the Phillies' American League rival—began luring away many of the team's top players. The impact on the Phillies was substantial. Three future Hall of Famers—second baseman Nap Lajoie, first baseman Ed Delahanty, and right fielder Elmer Flick—left the team, gutting a strong squad. No loss was greater than Lajoie, who hit .426 in his first season after leaving the Phillies, winning the first of three batting titles.

15 Nap Lajoie

The great second baseman played the first five years of his career with the Phillies before jumping to the rival Philadelphia Athletics, setting off a cantankerous chain of events. In 1902, Lajoie's second with the Athletics, the Phillies obtained an injunction that prohibited him from playing baseball for any team but the Phillies, but it was enforceable only in Pennsylvania. As a result, Lajoie's contract was transferred to Cleveland, where he became a fixture for more than a decade before eventually returning to Philadelphia—to join the Athletics, not the Phillies—at the end of his career. By that point, the injunction had been dismissed.

"LAJOIE WAS ONE OF THE MOST RUGGED HITTERS I EVER FACED. HE'D TAKE YOUR LEG OFF WITH A LINE DRIVE."

—Cy Young

16 The 20-Somethings

In 1901, the Phillies became the first 20th-century team to have three 20-game winners on its pitching staff. The trio of Al Orth, Red Donahue, and Bill Duggleby accomplished the feat—but with no room to spare. Each of the three pitchers won exactly 20 games. Having three 20-game winners remains a rare achievement. It has happened only 23 times in history—and it hasn't happened since the Oakland Athletics did it in 1973.

17 The Giant Killer

The 1908 season didn't have many shining moments for the Phillies, but near the end of the year, rookie left-hander Harry Coveleski provided a little sparkle. Over a period of six games, Coveleski beat the mighty New York Giants three times, costing the Giants a pennant and giving the Phillies and their fans something to smile about.

Al Orth

18 Billy Shettsline

Perhaps no one in the organization's long history has utilized the opportunity for advancement better than Shettsline. He did just about everything—except actually play for the Phillies. Shettsline started as a ticket taker at the Baker Bowl and eventually worked his way up to manager and team president. Shettsline was well liked in the early 1900s, but like many others in the franchise's history, he didn't have an inordinate amount of success as the team dealt with financial issues. There's even a story of Shettsline—who weighed more than 300 pounds—being chased off the field one day by a goat that the team had employed to help keep the outfield grass cut. As president, Shettsline decided to find a better solution than grazing livestock.

19 Horace Fogel

For a man whose reputation was built on being an astute baseball writer in his day, Fogel's career as a manager and owner didn't go very well. Before becoming the Phillies' owner in 1909, Fogel spent part of 1902 managing the New York Giants, where he unwisely tried to move the great young pitcher Christy Mathewson to first base, a move that was fortunately blunted. When he took over the Phillies as part of a business group that owned the club, Fogel tried to change the team's nickname to the Live Wires, even giving away trinkets with an emblem of an eagle holding sparking wires, but it didn't work. Fogel finally did himself in after the 1912 World Series by suggesting that during the regular season, St. Louis Cardinals manager Roger Bresnahan had intentionally not fielded his best players against the Giants, his former team, and the umpires had worked to ensure the Giants' victory. Unable to prove his statements to league officials, Fogel was banished from baseball because he had "undermined the integrity of the game."

20 1915

The Phillies' first World Series appearance started well—they won the first game, 3–1, against the Boston Red Sox—but didn't end so well. Boston won the next four games—all by a single run—and took the Series. The Phillies had posted a 90–62 record under manager Pat Moran and ridden the powerful pitching of Grover Cleveland Alexander to the National League pennant. Alexander won 31 games in 1915, pitching four one-hitters in the process and beating Boston's Ernie Shore in the Series opener. The Phillies also got a big season from Gavvy Cravath, who led the league with 24 home runs and 115 runs batted in. It wasn't enough, however, against a Boston team so loaded with talent that 20-year-old Babe Ruth's only appearance came as a pinch-hitter.

Left to right: Duffy Lewis, Ed Burns, Dutch Leonard, Gavvy Cravath, and Harry Hooper

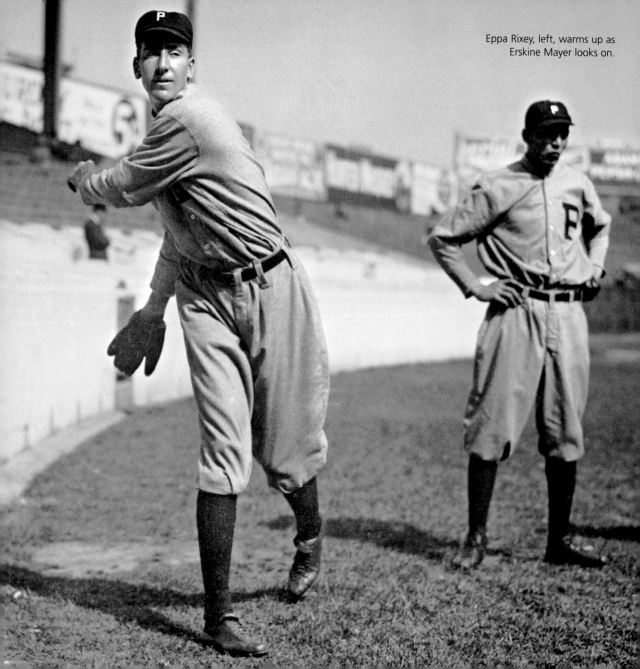

Eppa Rixey, left, warms up as
Erskine Mayer looks on.

21 Eppa Rixey

Rixey, a Hall of Famer, spent nine years with the Phillies at the start of his career, helping the team to its 1915 World Series appearance. He was tall—6 feet, 5 inches—and never pitched in the minors, a rarity. Known for his good nature—except when he lost—Rixey retired as the winningest left-handed pitcher in National League history with 266 victories, a number eventually passed by Warren Spahn of the Milwaukee Braves in 1959. During his career, Rixey acquired a middle name from a sportswriter who enjoyed the sound of putting "Jephtha" in between Eppa and Rixey. The pitcher liked it enough that he made it his middle name.

22 Dave Bancroft

Described as a classic shortstop, Dave "Beauty" Bancroft played six seasons, from 1915 to 1920, with the Phillies, part of a solid career that may be best known for his surprising induction into the National Baseball Hall of Fame. Bancroft was good at what he did but, by most accounts, not great. He hit .279 over his career and never had more than seven home runs in a season. He was, however, a favorite of former teammate Frankie Frisch, whose presence on the Hall's Veterans Committee may have secured Bancroft's induction.

"WHEN HE CAME TO THE PHILLIES FROM PORTLAND OF THE PACIFIC COAST LEAGUE, HE BROUGHT WITH HIM A HABIT OF SHOUTING 'BEAUTY' EVERY TIME HIS PITCHER SENT OVER A GOOD-LOOKING BALL. THAT'S THE HISTORY OF THE 'BEAUTY' HANDLE."

—Dan Daniel, the *New York Herald*, on Dave Bancroft

23 Grover Cleveland Alexander

By any measure, Alexander was one of the game's all-time great pitchers, and the best years in his career were spent with the Phillies. Alexander joined the Phillies in 1911, when his contract was purchased for $750. As a rookie, Alexander led the National League in wins (28), complete games (31), innings pitched (367), and shutouts (seven). His 16 shutouts in 1916 remain a single-season major-league record, and in three consecutive seasons, Alexander won 30 or more games. Alexander did it with a team that wasn't particularly good— his 190 wins in seven seasons were about one-third of the team's total at that time—and in a park that featured a right-field wall only 280 feet away.

24 Mr. President

Grover Cleveland Alexander had the distinction of being named after one president—he was born during the first term of Grover Cleveland—and later portrayed by a future president—Ronald Reagan—in the movie *The Winning Team.*

"HE IS THE ONE PLAYER IN OUR LEAGUE WHO COULD WIN THE PENNANT FOR ANY OF THE SEVEN TEAMS THAT WERE NOT IN FIRST PLACE."

—Bill Klem on Grover Cleveland Alexander

Grover Cleveland Alexander
and manager Pat Moran

25 Joe Oeschger's Long Day

On April 30, 1919, Oeschger pitched all 20 innings for the Phillies and at the end had nothing to show for it—the game ended in a 9–9 tie with the Brooklyn Dodgers. A year later—pitching for the Boston Braves—Oeschger pitched all 26 innings in what ended as a 1–1 tie with Brooklyn, whose pitcher, Leon Cadore, also went the distance. In the game, Oeschger pitched a record 21 consecutive scoreless innings.

26 Cy Williams

In the 13 seasons Williams played for the Phillies—from 1918 through 1930—the team didn't have much success, but it wasn't his fault. Williams won three National League home-run crowns in the 1920s while playing for the Phillies. He hit 15 in 1920, 41 in 1923, and 30 in 1927. The outfielder was the first National League player to hit 200 career home runs. He also had the distinction of having played football at Notre Dame with future coach Knute Rockne.

27 26–23

The score sounded more like a football game than a baseball game when the Phillies and Cubs were finished on August 25, 1922, in Chicago. The Cubs won, in part because they scored 14 runs in the fourth inning of what was the Phillies' fifth straight loss. The 49 total runs remain the most ever scored by two teams in a game, which also featured 51 hits, 23 walks, and 10 errors. Despite establishing the all-time record for runs scored, the two teams combined also left 25 men on base—a staggering number, all things considered. But then again, it was the Phillies and the Cubs.

Joe Oeschger

Crosley Field, May 24, 1935

28 Chuck Klein

Until Mike Schmidt came along, Chuck Klein was the man against whom the best hitters in Phillies history were measured. A left-handed slugger, Klein was able to take advantage of the short right-field wall in the Baker Bowl. For five consecutive seasons starting in 1929, Klein had at least 200 base hits, including a 250-hit season in 1930. He hit 300 career home runs (most of them while playing for the Phillies) and earned the 1932 National League MVP award. Not only could Klein hit, he was an outstanding outfielder. His 44 assists in 1930 remain a major-league record. Klein was inducted into the National Baseball Hall of Fame in 1980.

29 Hitting for Average

The 1930 Phillies were among the most dangerous hitting teams in the National League. Their .315 average remains the third highest in National League history. Unfortunately, everything else was a disaster. The Phillies lost 102 games that year, posting a team earned run average of 6.71. That happens when a team surrenders 1,199 runs in a season.

30 Lighting Up the Night

On May 24, 1935, the Phillies became part of history when they played the Cincinnati Reds at Crosley Field in the first night game ever. Some 600 miles away from Cincinnati, at the White House, President Franklin Delano Roosevelt flipped the ceremonial switch to light the ballpark, christening a new era in major-league sports. For the record, the Reds won, 2–1.

31 Shibe Park

Shibe Park opened in 1909 and was home to the Philadelphia Athletics, for whose owner, Ben Shibe, it was named. The Phillies played there for a portion of the 1927 season when their home park, the Baker Bowl, was damaged. The first steel and concrete stadium in the majors, Shibe Park became the Phillies' home in 1938. They shared the stadium with the A's until that team left for Kansas City after the 1954 season. In 1953, the park was renamed Connie Mack Stadium in honor of the Athletics' legendary manager. In 1956, the old scoreboard from Yankee Stadium was installed in the right-center-field wall. The Phillies played there until the end of the 1970 season; the following year the new Veterans Stadium awaited them. To honor their days at Shibe Park, the Phillies brought the home plate from their old park and installed it at the Vet.

Shibe Park, 1951

Robin Roberts and Bobby Shantz

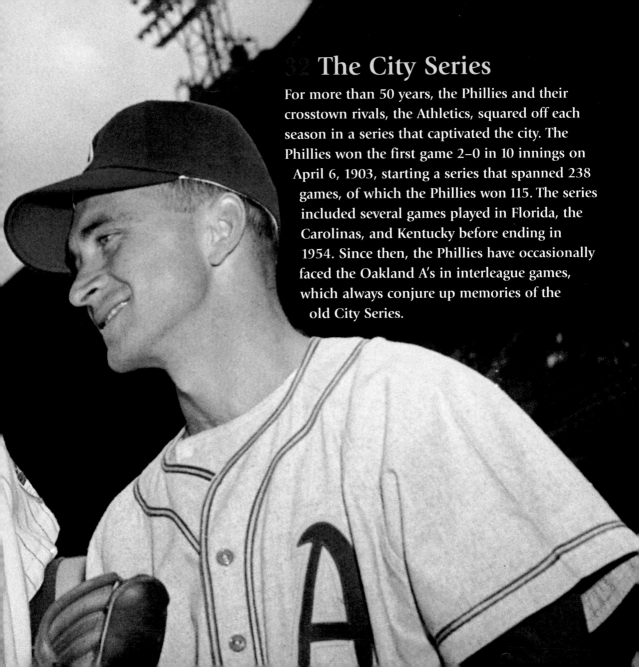

32 The City Series

For more than 50 years, the Phillies and their crosstown rivals, the Athletics, squared off each season in a series that captivated the city. The Phillies won the first game 2–0 in 10 innings on April 6, 1903, starting a series that spanned 238 games, of which the Phillies won 115. The series included several games played in Florida, the Carolinas, and Kentucky before ending in 1954. Since then, the Phillies have occasionally faced the Oakland A's in interleague games, which always conjure up memories of the old City Series.

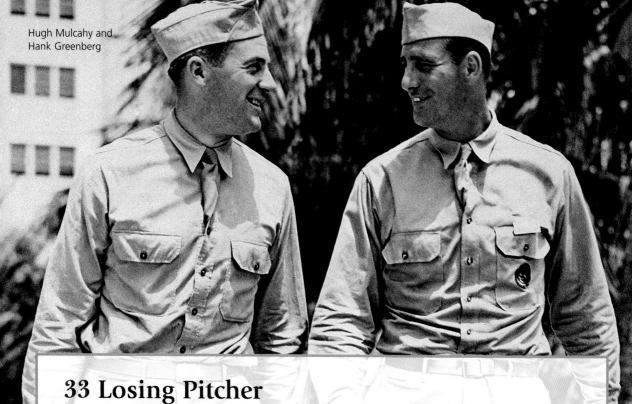

Hugh Mulcahy and
Hank Greenberg

33 Losing Pitcher

That's what fans and writers nicknamed Phillies pitcher Hugh Mulcahy—and it fit.
Mulcahy was a workhorse, but he didn't have a lot of success, in part because the
team he pitched for wasn't loaded with much talent. He pitched nine years in the
majors—the first eight with the Phillies—and, like his team, never won more
games than he lost. In fact, his career record was 45–89, and he led the National
League in losses with 20 in 1938 and 22 in 1940. Despite his numbers in those
two years, Mulcahy still managed to finish among the top 30 vote getters in MVP
balloting. Mulcahy had another distinction besides his nickname: In 1941, he
became the first major-league player drafted into the army during World War II.

34 The Golden Glove

Outfielder Danny Litwhiler was a solid player for the Phillies during the early part of his 11-year career, and he achieved a bit of baseball history in 1942 when he became the first player to handle every fielding chance perfectly over an entire season. Litwhiler had no errors on 317 chances. The feat was so remarkable that years after he retired, the National Baseball Hall of Fame asked for his glove and has it on display in Cooperstown, New York.

35 The Not-So-Golden Years

The Phillies and their fans are no strangers to losing. But few stretches have ever matched the dubious mark achieved from 1938 through the 1942 season, when the Phillies lost at least 100 games in five consecutive seasons.

36 William Cox

When Cox, a former Yale baseball player, bought the Phillies in 1943 at the young age of 33, he promised to finally pump money into a franchise that had historically struggled due to a lack of financing. At last there was reason for optimism. He hired manager Bucky Harris, who had taken the Washington Senators to two World Series, and immediately invested in upgrading the franchise. The good news didn't last long, however. Harris didn't like the owner's hands-on approach, and Cox fired his manager in July. What he didn't know was that Harris had found out Cox had been betting on the Phillies in violation of major-league rules. When word got out and an investigation proved the accusations to be true, Commissioner Kenesaw Mountain Landis banned Cox from baseball for life—the second Phillies' owner to be so banished.

37 At Home in Clearwater

Since 1948, the Phillies have made Clearwater, Florida, their spring-training destination. It's a beautiful spot to go to work on a new season, close by the Gulf of Mexico. For nearly 50 years, the Phillies played their spring-training games in Jack Russell Stadium, but that was replaced in 2004 by Bright House Networks Field, one of the finest spring-training facilities in the majors. The park has a capacity of 8,500 and classic Florida-style architecture. Palm trees tower behind the outfield walls, and beyond left field there's a tiki hut, which allows more than 200 fans to watch the game in an island-like setting. The park also serves as home to the Class A Clearwater Threshers.

38 Sparky Anderson

It's no secret that Anderson's baseball legend was built as a manager, not as a player. He was the first manager to win the World Series with one team each from the National and American Leagues, and he ranks fifth all-time in victories among managers. Anderson played only one full season in the majors—1959 with the Phillies. He was a second baseman who was solid in the field but not much at the plate. Anderson hit .218 in his only major-league season and figured out quickly that his future was in the dugout, not on the field.

Left: Ryan Howard signs autographs at spring training in Clearwater.

39 Richie Ashburn

When the great names in Phillies history are listed, Ashburn always ranks near the top. For 12 years, he played center field and batted leadoff for the Phillies, coming to represent the franchise. Ashburn was a classic singles hitter; in fact, 86 percent of his 2,574 career base hits were singles. He batted .300 or better nine times in his career, twice winning batting titles. Power wasn't part of Ashburn's game—he hit just 29 home runs in his career—but he maximized his talents. When his playing days ended, Ashburn became a Phillies radio announcer in 1963 and made a second career in broadcasting until he died in 1997.

40 Alice Roth's Tough Day

Alice Roth, the wife of *Philadelphia Bulletin* sports editor Earl Roth, was sitting in the box seats along the third base line at Connie Mack Stadium on August 17, 1957, when a foul ball off the bat of Phillies star Richie Ashburn hit her in the face, breaking her nose. The game was momentarily delayed while medical attention was directed to Roth, and she was placed on a stretcher. When play resumed, Ashburn fouled off another pitch, which also caught Roth in the face as she was being carried out of the ballpark.

"TO CURE A BATTING SLUMP,
I TOOK MY BAT TO BED WITH ME.
I WANTED TO KNOW MY BAT
A LITTLE BETTER."

—Richie Ashburn

41 The Whiz Kids

When the Phillies transformed themselves from cellar dwellers to contenders in the 1950s, they did it with a nucleus of young players known as "the Whiz Kids." Future Hall of Famers Richie Ashburn and pitcher Robin Roberts were key elements on a roster that in 1950 delivered the franchise its first National League pennant in 35 years. Owner Bob Carpenter deserves some of the credit for agreeing to invest in the club's farm system with the intention of developing fresh, young talent. It paid off with stars such as Ashburn, Roberts, Del Ennis, Granny Hamner, Willie Jones, Curt Simmons, and others. The story the Whiz Kids wrote in 1950 remains among the most endearing in Phillies history.

42 Dick Sisler's Home Run

Life had turned grim for the Phillies when they arrived at Ebbets Field to play the Brooklyn Dodgers in the final regular-season game in 1950. Their seven-game lead was down to one when they put ace Robin Roberts on the mound for the critical game. Roberts did his part by limiting the Dodgers to one run, but it wasn't easy. In the bottom of the ninth, Richie Ashburn threw out Brooklyn's Cal Abrams at the plate, which prevented a winning run and sent the game into extra innings. In the tenth, Dick Sisler cemented the pennant for the Phillies when he slammed an opposite-field, three-run homer, which remains among the most memorable moments in team history. It was one of only 55 home runs Sisler hit in his eight-year career.

Dick Sisler (8) receives congratulations from teammates.

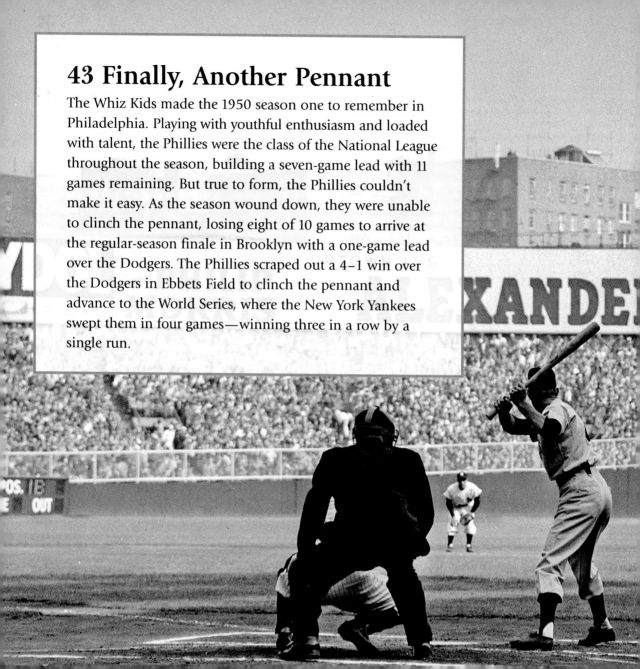

43 Finally, Another Pennant

The Whiz Kids made the 1950 season one to remember in Philadelphia. Playing with youthful enthusiasm and loaded with talent, the Phillies were the class of the National League throughout the season, building a seven-game lead with 11 games remaining. But true to form, the Phillies couldn't make it easy. As the season wound down, they were unable to clinch the pennant, losing eight of 10 games to arrive at the regular-season finale in Brooklyn with a one-game lead over the Dodgers. The Phillies scraped out a 4–1 win over the Dodgers in Ebbets Field to clinch the pennant and advance to the World Series, where the New York Yankees swept them in four games—winning three in a row by a single run.

The Yankees' Eddie Lopat pitches to Eddie
Waitkus in Game 3 of the 1950 World Series.

Robin Roberts

44 Robin Roberts

Roberts was among the defining pitchers of his generation, using control to become one of the most successful pitchers ever. Part of the famous Whiz Kids, Roberts was the horse of the staff in 1950. He started the final game of the regular season, limiting the Brooklyn Dodgers to one run in a game the Phillies had to win. It was Roberts' third start in five days. From 1950 through 1955, Roberts won at least 20 games every season, topping out with 28 wins in 1952. A seven-time All-Star, he once pitched 28 complete games in a row. Roberts retired with a 286–245 career record, with 305 complete games and 45 shutouts, having spent the bulk of his career with the Phillies. He was elected to the National Baseball Hall of Fame in 1976.

"PROBABLY THE BEST FASTBALL I EVER SAW WAS ROBIN ROBERTS'.... HIS BALL WOULD RISE AROUND SIX OR EIGHT INCHES, AND WITH PLENTY ON IT. AND HE HAD GREAT CONTROL, WHICH MADE HIM VERY DIFFICULT TO HIT."

—Ralph Kiner

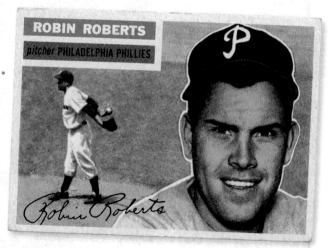

45 Del Ennis

Born in Philadelphia, Ennis was a key member of the Whiz Kids. He could hit with power, and for a time he was the franchise's all-time leader in games played and home runs. During the 1950 season, Ennis hit .311 with 31 home runs and 126 runs batted in. By 1956, he ranked among the top 10 home-run hitters of all time in the National League. Ennis had a fickle relationship with the Philadelphia fans, who loved him for his power but often tormented him for his mistakes. He finished with a .284 career batting average, 2,063 hits, and 288 home runs. Ennis' 1,284 runs batted in from 1946 through 1959 were the second-highest total in the National League during that period, behind Stan Musial.

46 Jim Konstanty

For all the chatter through the years about the Whiz Kids, the true star of the 1950 Phillies turned out to be a veteran relief pitcher named Jim Konstanty. He pitched for five teams during his 13-year career, but it was 1950 when Konstanty became a hero. Setting a major-league record by appearing in 74 games, Konstanty was named the National League Most Valuable Player after winning 16 games and picking up 22 saves. In Game 1 of the World Series, Konstanty held the New York Yankees to four hits but lost, 1–0.

Jim Konstanty pitches to Gene
Woodling in the 1950 World Series.
Inset: Del Ennis

Giants manager Leo Durocher, left, and Eddie Sawyer shake hands with General Douglas MacArthur, center.

47 Eddie Sawyer's Sudden Good-bye

Sawyer had the good fortune of managing the Phillies during the Whiz Kids days, leading the team to the 1950 National League pennant. The good days didn't last long, however, and in 1952 Sawyer was fired as the team's fortunes flagged. Six years later, when things hadn't improved, the Phillies rehired Sawyer, but there was no magic as the team finished last in 1958 and again in 1959. Still the manager when the 1960 season began, Sawyer sat through the Phillies' season opener—a 9–4 loss to the Cincinnati Reds—and immediately announced his retirement by saying, "I'm 49 years old, and I want to live to be 50."

48 *The Old Man and the Sea*

In Ernest Hemingway's classic short novel *The Old Man and the Sea*, the fishermen Santiago and Manolin occasionally discuss baseball. They talk about the 1950 pennant races and the players involved, leading to Santiago's reminiscing about Dick Sisler, whom he had seen play in Cuba.

"In the other league, between Brooklyn and Philadelphia, I must take Brooklyn," Santiago said. "But then I think of Dick Sisler and those great drives in the old park.

"There was nothing ever like them. He hits the longest ball I've ever seen."

49 23 in a Row

To become the first—and so far only—franchise to lose 10,000 games, there have to be some really bad stretches. And there have been. But nothing has equaled the Phillies' 23-game losing streak in 1961. How long did it last? From July 29 until August 20. And thank goodness for pitcher John Buzhardt. He was the winning pitcher when the Phillies beat San Francisco in the game before the losing streak began, and he went the distance on August 20 to end the 23-game nightmare.

JOHN BUZHARDT
Pitcher

Philadelphia
Phillies

"EVERYBODY IN THE LEAGUE WAS BEATING US."
—John Buzhardt

Johnny Callison homers in
the 1964 All-Star Game.

50 Johnny Callison

Throughout the decade of the 1960s, Callison came to symbolize the Phillies. An exceptional outfielder, Callison had one of the most feared arms in baseball, daring runners to take an extra base against him. He was also a powerful hitter, finishing his career among the top five Phillies home-run hitters up to then. Callison was a three-time All-Star, leading outfielders in assists for four straight seasons. He hit for the cycle against Pittsburgh on June 7, 1963, and finished second in the MVP voting in 1964, the same year he was named MVP of the All-Star Game after hitting the game-winning home run.

51 Callison's All-Star Moment

In a season that would end in bitter disappointment for the Phillies, the 1964 All-Star Game remained a sparkling moment. It was played in New York's Shea Stadium, and the National and American Leagues were tied 4–4 in the bottom of the ninth, with two men on base and two out. The Phillies' Johnny Callison stepped to the plate to face dangerous Dick Radatz. Callison then slammed the game-winning three-run homer that helped define his career. It also made Callison one of only three players—Ted Williams and Stan Musial are the others—to hit walk-off game-winning home runs in the All-Star Game.

Jim Bunning pitching a perfect game against the Mets

52 Jim Bunning

A Hall of Famer, Bunning played for four teams in his career, but he's best known for his days with the Phillies from 1964 through 1967 and again in 1970–71. A big, strong right-hander, Bunning won 19 games in each of three consecutive years for the Phillies, from 1964 through 1966. In his 17-year career, Bunning was a nine-time All-Star and one of only five pitchers to throw a no-hitter in both the American and National Leagues. When Bunning left baseball, he went home to Kentucky, where he was elected to the House of Representatives and is now in his second term as a United States senator.

53 The Perfect Game

On Father's Day, June 21, 1964, Jim Bunning pitched one of only 17 perfect games ever recorded in the majors. He did it against the New York Mets, winning 6–0, becoming the first National League pitcher in 84 years to throw a perfect game. Bunning was economical that day, throwing just 90 pitches, 79 of which were strikes. The story goes that in the ninth inning, aware of the enormity of the moment, Bunning called catcher Gus Triandos to the mound and asked him to tell a joke to break the tension. Triandos couldn't think of one and, instead, just laughed at Bunning. After completing his perfect game, Bunning appeared that evening on *The Ed Sullivan Show*.

Richie Allen

54 Richie Allen

There haven't been many in Philadelphia—or anywhere else—quite like Richie "Call Me Dick" Allen. He was an extraordinary talent, a man with immense power at a time when pitchers seemed to rule baseball. But Allen, who was Rookie of the Year when he broke in with the Phillies in 1964, seemed to be forever involved in one controversy or another. After six full seasons in Philly, Allen was traded to St. Louis. He eventually wound up back with the Phillies, though it was never a happy marriage. Fans yelled at him, and he took to wearing a helmet in the field in case anything was thrown at him. To make his unhappiness apparent, Allen once scratched "Trade Me" in the infield dirt while playing first base in a home game. One could argue that Allen deserves Hall of Fame consideration, especially with a .534 career slugging percentage. He was never chosen to join the Hall of Fame, but his impact on Philadelphia may be everlasting.

"ALLEN WAS SCARY AT THE PLATE.... I WANT TO FORGET A COUPLE OF LINE DRIVES HE HIT OFF ME, BUT I CAN'T BECAUSE THEY ALMOST KILLED ME."

—Mickey Lolich

55 Gene Mauch

No man has ever managed more major-league games without winning a pennant than Gene Mauch. And the one that got away happened in Philadelphia in 1964, when Mauch's Phillies couldn't capture a pennant they had seemed destined to win. As a player, Mauch was a solid utility infielder who was never a starter, playing in spots and studying the game. He believed baseball was best played with good pitching, strong defense, and sharp fundamentals. It's how he wanted all the teams he managed to play—and they generally did, though they were never quite good enough, three times coming within a game of winning a pennant. Mauch's face as the Phillies collapsed in 1964 remains an eternal image among Philadelphia fans.

DICK ALLEN REMEMBERS • MAUCH GETS A BLACK EYE
CHICO RUIZ STEALS HOME (AGAIN) • WHERE ARE THEY NOW?

PhillySport

JUNE 1989 $2

TWENTY-FIVE YEARS LATER

'64

WILL WE
EVER
FORGET?

Philly Skipper
Gene Mauch

56 The Phold

It couldn't happen—but it did. With 12 games remaining in the 1964 season, the Phillies had a 6 1/2-game lead in the National League—with their next seven games at home. World Series tickets were printed. But all that had come so easily for the Phillies through the season—a year when Richie Allen was Rookie of the Year—went bad. The Phillies lost 10 games in a row and surrendered first place to the St. Louis Cardinals. Jim Bunning and Chris Short, the stars of the pitching staff, worked on two days' rest, and it showed. The bats cooled. Strategy backfired. Pressure mounted. And then it was gone. It was a nightmare come to life. It was, in a bitter way, the story of a franchise.

"IF IT'S TRUE THAT WE LEARN FROM ADVERSITY,
THEN I'M THE SMARTEST SON OF A BITCH ON EARTH."
—Gene Mauch

57 Chico Ruiz Steals Home

When the autopsy was done on the Phillies' 1964 collapse, it all started with Cincinnati's Chico Ruiz. The Phillies had a 61/2-game lead with 12 games remaining when Ruiz suddenly stole home in the sixth inning of a scoreless game, with Reds slugger Frank Robinson at the plate. It was a shocking play and produced the game's only run, starting the Phillies on a fateful 10-game losing streak.

58 Tony Taylor

He was among the most beloved Phillies of any generation. An infielder who primarily played second base, Taylor was a fixture in Philly from 1960 through 1971, and he returned to finish his career with the Phillies in the mid-1970s. Taylor was solid in every area, earning a spot on the Phillies' Wall of Fame. He played a record 1,003 games at second base for the Phillies and owns the distinction of having stolen home six times. Taylor also made the play that saved Jim Bunning's perfect game in 1964, knocking down Jesse Gonder's line shot between first and second and throwing him out in the fifth inning.

PHILADELPHIA PHILLIES

"IT WAS A GREAT PLAY. WHEN HE DID THAT, I KNEW I HAD SOMETHING SPECIAL."

—Jim Bunning on Tony Taylor

"A GRACEFUL INFIELDER WHO WAS POPULAR WITH FANS."

—TheBaseballPage.com on Tony Taylor

Curt Flood pauses in front of federal court in New York City, 1970.

59 Curt Flood

He didn't want to play for the Phillies, and he went to the U.S. Supreme Court to prove it. Flood, an excellent center fielder, was traded from the St. Louis Cardinals along with catcher Tim McCarver, outfielder Byron Browne, and pitcher Joe Hoerner to the Phillies for first baseman Dick Allen, second baseman Cookie Rojas, and pitcher Jerry Johnson prior to the 1970 season. Flood, however, with the help of the players' union, challenged the validity of baseball's "reserve clause." Forfeiting a $100,000 salary, Flood sat out the 1970 season while the matter went to court. Eventually, the Supreme Court sided with baseball commissioner Bowie Kuhn and let the reserve clause stand. Flood, meanwhile, was traded to the Washington Senators, where he played briefly in 1971 before retiring—but not without ultimately making a dramatic impact on the game.

60 The Swingin' Seventies

Finally, after decades of disappointment, the Phillies found a way to win in the 1970s. It didn't start well—the Phillies won just 59 games in 1972—but with a lineup that would become the foundation of their first world championship, in 1980, the Phillies were on their way. They won three straight National League East titles beginning in 1976. Although they never made it to the World Series—losing playoff series to the Reds in 1976 and to the Dodgers in 1977 and 1978—the Phillies had turned an emotional corner in the direction of the franchise.

"BASEBALL WAS SOCIALLY RELEVANT, AND SO WAS MY REBELLION AGAINST IT."

—Curt Flood

61 The Vet

Built in an era when round, multipurpose facilities were in vogue, Veterans Stadium served as the Phillies' home from 1971 through the 2003 season. The stadium itself didn't have much personality—it looked like so many other stadiums built around the same time—but it had life when the Phillies were there. The artificial-turf field was considered the worst in the majors and the fans upstairs in the 700 level among the most vociferous in any sport. But it was where Mike Schmidt's legend was built, where Tug McGraw threw the final pitch of the 1980 World Series victory, and where two All-Star games (1976 and 1996) were played. Situated on the corner of Broad Street and Pattison Avenue, the Vet was where Terry Mulholland and Kevin Millwood each pitched a no-hitter against the San Francisco Giants. And if you're in the parking lot at the new Citizens Bank Park, you can find a monument marking the spot where home plate was in the old Vet.

62 The Phillie Phanatic

Nothing says Phillies baseball quite like an oversized, clumsy, fuzzy green creature with a big nose and a tongue that pops in and out. It's crazy, but it's true. Many feel the Phanatic is the best mascot in sports—and they're not all from Philadelphia. Created in the 1970s as an answer to San Diego's famous Chicken, the Phanatic has become a part of major-league baseball. He rides an ATV, chides opposing teams, wears a star on his back, and makes sure everyone has a good time. And he's a whole lot more fun than Philadelphia Phil and Philadelphia Phyllis, the two 18th-century characters he replaced.

The Phillie Phanatic peers over the roof of Veterans Stadium.

63 The Stuntman

During the many years when Bill Giles ran the Phillies, entertainment was often part of the game experience. They held ostrich races and duck races on the field—without much success. They had Kurt Wallenda perform his tightrope act across the top of the stadium, stopping to do a handstand over the middle of the field. But few, if any, stunts matched the Kiteman in 1972. The idea was to have a man bring the ball for opening day into Veterans Stadium using what amounted to a hang glider. It took some searching, but Giles found a man named Richard Johnson who was willing to try it for $1,500. He strapped on a pair of water skis and, with the game ball taped to him, attempted to ski down a specially built ramp in the upper deck of the stadium. Unfortunately, a gust of wind knocked the Kiteman off the ramp before he could get airborne. He gathered himself, pulled the ball free, and flung it toward the field to start a season that would produce just 59 victories.

Kurt Wallenda walks a tightrope across Veterans Stadium, 1972.

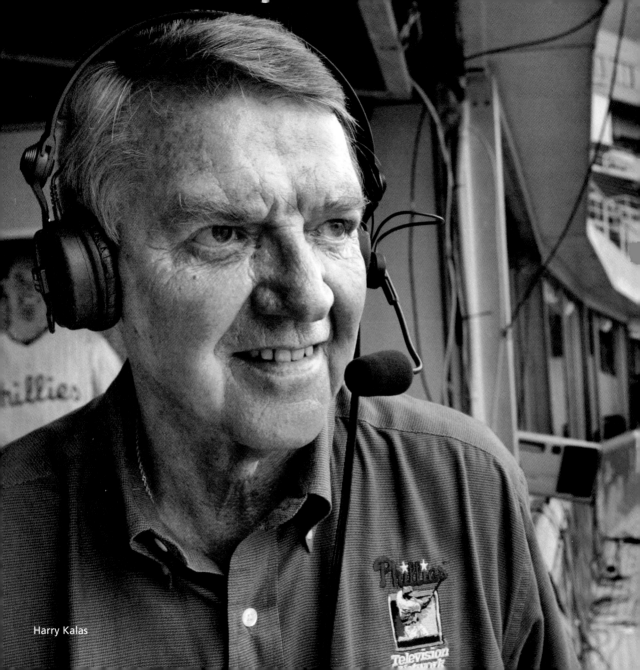

Harry Kalas

64 A Fashion Statement

Through the years, the Phillies have often altered their uniforms, their caps, and their logos. But in 1977, the Phillies changed the way baseball teams dressed. In that season—and keep in mind, the '70s aren't remembered for the fashion they produced—the Phillies became the first team to wear special batting-practice jerseys. It was a maroon, V-necked shirt with "Phillies" across the front and the player's name and number across the back. Unlike the other fashions of that time, this one didn't go away.

However, not every idea is a good one. For more than 20 years, the Phillies wore burgundy as their primary color rather than red, and one Saturday night team officials took the idea a little too far. During the 1979 season, the Phillies showed up for a Saturday night game wearing all-burgundy uniforms with white trim. It was not a good look. The players didn't like them. The fans didn't like them. The media made fun of them. Fortunately, like many other bad clothing designs in the '70s, the uniforms—called "Saturday Night Specials"—quickly disappeared.

65 The Voices

There have been many through the years, but three have been the nearest and dearest to Phillies fans: By Saam, Richie Ashburn, and Harry Kalas. Saam began calling Phillies games in 1939, one year after he started with the rival Philadelphia Athletics. He left the Phillies booth before the 1950 season but returned in 1955 and stayed through 1975, having called more than 4,000 losses between the two Philadelphia teams. Ashburn's legend was made on the field, but he remained a part of the franchise with his work in the booth, where he broadcast for 27 seasons alongside Kalas, whose voice and style have become instantly recognizable.

"I DON'T THINK
I CAN GET INTO MY
DEEP INNER THOUGHTS
ABOUT HITTING.
IT'S LIKE TALKING
ABOUT RELIGION."

—Mike Schmidt

66 Mike Schmidt

He has been called the best third baseman in history by many, and they're probably right. Beyond what he did on the field—and that was plenty—Schmidt was the face of sports in Philadelphia during much of the 1970s and 1980s. He was the definition of a tough guy on the field, and his intensity practically glowed. Schmidt hit 548 home runs and drove in 1,595 runs, earning a spot in the starting lineup when Major League Baseball named its All-Century Team in 1999. He was a three-time National League MVP, a 12-time All-Star, and 10-time Gold Glove winner. In the 1980s, *The Sporting News* named him the player of the decade. Schmidt is at the top of the list in most offensive categories for the Phillies, including home runs, RBI, games played (2,404), runs scored (1,506), and hits (2,234). His number, 20, has been retired by the Phillies, and he was elected to the National Baseball Hall of Fame in 1995. That's why he's considered the best third baseman ever to play the game.

67 Outta Here—Times Four

Only 15 players have hit four home runs in the same game, and Michael Jack Schmidt put his name on that list on April 17, 1976, in a game against the Chicago Cubs. Schmidt was in the prime of his career, and his power was extraordinary. He was in the midst of an extraordinary start—hitting 12 home runs in the first 15 games of the 1976 season to set a record eventually tied by Alex Rodriguez—when he punished the Cubs. Not only did Schmidt hit four home runs in the game, he did it in consecutive at bats.

68 Danny Ozark

Ozark did what few others had been able to do—he brought a winner to Philadelphia. There was work to be done when Ozark took over in 1973, and the improvement started quickly. By 1976, the Phillies had won a franchise-record 101 games in the Bicentennial year, before running into Cincinnati's "Big Red Machine" in the postseason. Ozark's Phillies won three straight division titles starting in 1976, amassing 292 regular-season victories in that stretch—but they never reached the World Series.

"HALF THIS GAME IS NINETY PERCENT MENTAL."

—Danny Ozark

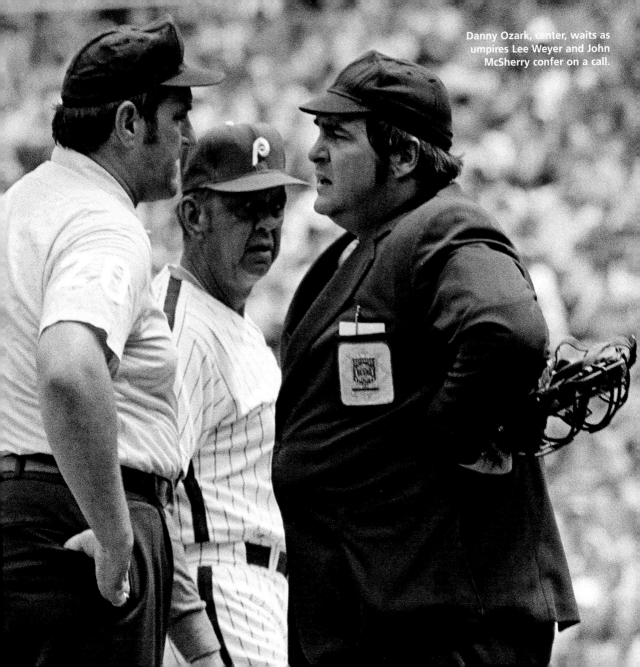

Danny Ozark, center, waits as umpires Lee Weyer and John McSherry confer on a call.

69 Steve Carlton

Lefty, as fans came to know him, was more than a left-handed pitcher. He was a force of nature. When Steve Carlton took the mound, the game changed. With a slider that could embarrass the best hitters in the game and a will just as devastating, Carlton remains one of the greatest pitchers in baseball history. Pitching for the Phillies from 1972 into 1986, Carlton became the first pitcher to win four Cy Young awards (1972, 1977, 1980, and 1982). He famously avoided speaking to the media, adding to the air of mystery that surrounded him and his workouts, which included martial arts and burying his fist in a large bucket of rice. For a time, Carlton was baseball's all-time strikeout leader, before surrendering the distinction to Nolan Ryan. With 4,136 strikeouts and 329 victories, it was little wonder that Carlton received 96 percent of the votes in his first year on the Hall of Fame ballot.

70 The One-Man Team

The 1972 Phillies won just 59 games, but, remarkably, Steve Carlton was the winning pitcher in 27 of them. Not only was it the last time a National League pitcher won 25 or more games in a season, it was easily the highest percentage of a team's total regular-season wins that any pitcher has ever had. Carlton finished with a 27–10 record that season while leading the National League in every major statistical category. He won 15 straight games, threw eight shutouts, and pitched 30 complete games while pitching 346 1/3 innings.

"LEFTY WAS A CRAFTSMAN, AN ARTIST.... HE PAINTED A BALLGAME. STROKE, STROKE, STROKE, AND WHEN HE GOT THROUGH IT WAS A MASTERPIECE."

—Richie Ashburn
on Steve Carlton

71 Rick Wise's Big Day

Phillies pitcher Rick Wise threw a no-hitter against the Cincinnati Reds in Riverfront Stadium on June 23, 1971. But that's just part of the story. Wise made his career day more memorable by hitting two home runs in the game—the only time in the history of major-league baseball a pitcher has homered twice while tossing a no-hitter. And it wasn't entirely a fluke. Later in the season, Wise had another two-homer game, this time against the San Francisco Giants. Also later that year, Wise retired 32 consecutive batters in a 12-inning game in which he drove in the winning run.

72 Tony Lucadello

Before players can become stars, they have to be discovered. That was the genius of longtime Phillies scout Tony Lucadello. He found and signed dozens of major leaguers for the Phillies, including Mike Schmidt, who hit just .179 with one home run as a high-school senior. But Lucadello, who had watched Schmidt since he was a Little Leaguer, believed in the prospect. Lucadello believed most of baseball was played from the waist down, and he spent extra time studying which players used their legs and feet. He was a great believer in fundamentals and was instrumental in developing a Major League Baseball instructional video that helped spread the game worldwide.

"THE AMAZING THING WAS HOW HE HELPED HIMSELF WITH THE BAT. I MEAN TO PITCH A NO-HITTER IS ONE THING, BUT TO HIT NOT ONE BUT TWO HOMERS IS UNBELIEVABLE."

—Harry Kalas on Rick Wise

Rick Wise accepting the Life Saver
of the Month trophy in 1971

"LARRY BOWA IS THE BEST SHORTSTOP I'VE EVER SEEN."

—Davey Johnson

73 Larry Bowa

The Phillies' shortstop from 1970 through 1981—and later their manager—Bowa was as tough as they come. He had a temper and a tenacity that marked his career as a player and, later, as a manager. Bowa wasn't a great hitter, but he was an exceptional fielder, handling shortstop as few others ever have. When Bowa retired after the 1985 season, he was the all-time leader in games played by a National League shortstop (2,222), and his .980 career fielding percentage was the highest ever by a shortstop. From 2001 through 2004, Bowa returned to manage the Phillies.

74 The DeJesus Trade

Baseball's history is cluttered with dozens of bad deals and a handful of really awful trades. Boston traded Babe Ruth to New York for cash. Remember Frank Robinson for Milt Pappas? Doyle Alexander for John Smoltz? Then there was the Phillies-Cubs trade on January 27, 1982, which sent Phillies five-time All-Star shortstop Larry Bowa to Chicago for shortstop Ivan DeJesus. And, just to make sure the Cubs felt good about the deal, the Phillies threw in a young second baseman named Ryne Sandberg. All he did was become a 10-time All-Star, win nine Gold Gloves, and establish himself as one of the best players of his generation. DeJesus lasted three forgettable seasons in Philadelphia, was traded to the Cardinals in 1985, and played for four other teams before calling it a career.

81

Larry Bowa leaps over the Expos' Jerry White.

75 The Bull

Greg Luzinski exuded raw power when he stepped to the plate, and he had a knack for delivering the big blow. While the Phillies were winning four National League East titles in five years through the late 1970s into 1980, Luzinski was the other half of a homer-hammering duo with Mike Schmidt. For six consecutive seasons, they combined to average 66 home runs a year, giving the Phillies a ferocious one-two punch. Luzinski, who earned his nickname from his immense stature, smacked 39 homers in 1977, to go along with 130 RBI and a .309 batting average, all career highs. The Bull wasn't a graceful outfielder, and he struck out regularly, but the fans loved him.

76 The 1976 All-Star Game

It was the nation's Bicentennial year—where else would you play the All-Star Game but Philly? President Gerald Ford threw out the first pitch, and former Phillies great Robin Roberts was an honorary member of the National League team. The National League won, 7–1, and Cincinnati's George Foster won the MVP award. In a touch of irony, one of the American League coaches was Gene Mauch, who had managed the infamous 1964 Phillies. The star of the game, however, was a quirky rookie pitcher from the Detroit Tigers named Mark Fidrych, who liked to talk to himself during the game. When it was over, everyone was talking about him.

President Gerald Ford and
Commissioner Bowie Kuhn
at the 1976 All-Star Game
Inset: Greg Luzinski

Pete Rose slides into home as the Cardinals' Darrell Porter attempts to tag him out.

77 Pete Rose

When the Phillies lured Rose away from Cincinnati's "Big Red Machine" prior to the 1979 season with a four-year, $3.2 million contract, they did it because they believed he could provide the missing piece in a franchise desperately seeking a World Series championship.

While Rose temporarily was the highest-paid player in team sports, the Phillies became World Champions in 1980, his second year with the team. Rose certainly did his part, too. In addition to the unparalleled leadership and experience he provided, he hit well, batting over .300 in 1979 and 1981, and played nearly flawless first base for the Phillies.

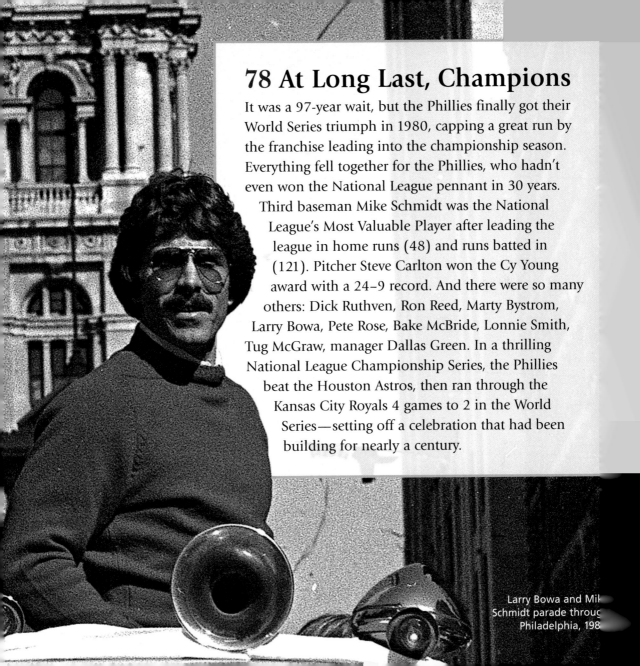

78 At Long Last, Champions

It was a 97-year wait, but the Phillies finally got their World Series triumph in 1980, capping a great run by the franchise leading into the championship season. Everything fell together for the Phillies, who hadn't even won the National League pennant in 30 years.

Third baseman Mike Schmidt was the National League's Most Valuable Player after leading the league in home runs (48) and runs batted in (121). Pitcher Steve Carlton won the Cy Young award with a 24–9 record. And there were so many others: Dick Ruthven, Ron Reed, Marty Bystrom, Larry Bowa, Pete Rose, Bake McBride, Lonnie Smith, Tug McGraw, manager Dallas Green. In a thrilling National League Championship Series, the Phillies beat the Houston Astros, then ran through the Kansas City Royals 4 games to 2 in the World Series—setting off a celebration that had been building for nearly a century.

Larry Bowa and Mik
Schmidt parade throug
Philadelphia, 198

"THEY SAY THAT WAS THE SLOWEST FASTBALL EVER THROWN IN PHILADELPHIA. IT TOOK 97 YEARS TO GET THERE."

—Tug McGraw

Tug McGraw and Mike Schmidt celebrate winning the 1980 World Series.

79 Willie Wilson Strikes Out

The moment had been building for almost 100 years, and it came down to Philadelphia relief pitcher Tug McGraw on the mound looking in at Kansas City outfielder Willie Wilson, the last man between the Phillies and their elusive world championship. Veterans Stadium seemed to shake with noise and anticipation. The Phillies led 4–1, but the bases were loaded and McGraw had been struggling. He'd walked three batters in the ninth inning of Game 5, a 4–3 Philadelphia victory, and now McGraw had allowed the Royals to load the bases three times in the eighth and ninth innings of Game 6. But helped by Pete Rose's dramatic catch of a Frank White pop-up that bounced out of catcher Bob Boone's glove for the second out, McGraw delivered the championship when he struck out Wilson—who fanned 12 times in the Series.

80 Tug McGraw

His name was Frank Edwin McGraw, Jr., but the world knew him as Tug. He was a two-time All-Star who originally starred for the New York Mets, then wound up in Philadelphia, where he helped the Phillies win the 1980 World Series. The photograph of McGraw standing on the pitching mound after the final out of the 1980 Series remains one of the iconic images in franchise history. He wasn't just a pitcher. He was a character, even while saving 20 games and compiling a 1.46 earned run average in 1980. It was McGraw who said, "Ninety percent (of my salary) I'll spend on good times, women, and Irish whiskey. The other 10 percent I'll probably waste." And one other thing—his kid, Tim McGraw, turned out to be a pretty good country singer.

81 The Secretary of Defense

Few nicknames have been more appropriate than the one given to Phillies center fielder Garry Maddox, who made fielding an art. Maddox was traded to the Phillies from San Francisco in 1975 and spent the next 11 seasons swallowing fly balls, cutting off balls hit into the gap, and daring runners to take the extra base on him. With enough speed to steal 248 career bases, Maddox could get to balls other outfielders might not, and his glove was one of the surest bets in baseball. Maddox won eight straight Gold Glove awards starting in 1975, but his greatest honor may have come in 1986 when he won the prestigious Roberto Clemente award, honoring him for his work in the community and for helping the underprivileged.

82 The Wheeze Kids

In 1983, just three years removed from their world championship, the Phillies again found themselves in the World Series. Suddenly, it was becoming routine. Even many of the faces were the same—Mike Schmidt, Steve Carlton, Pete Rose, Garry Maddox—along with future Hall of Famer Joe Morgan, who had arrived via trade. But age had begun to creep up on these Phillies, earning them the nickname "the Wheeze Kids," a play on the Whiz Kids of the 1950s. They won the NL pennant, but the Baltimore Orioles left with the World Series championship trophy.

"TWO-THIRDS OF THE EARTH IS COVERED BY WATER. THE REST IS COVERED BY GARRY MADDOX."

—Harry Kalas

Garry Maddox
receives congratulations
from his teammates.

83 Von Hayes Double Dips

Forget whether the five-for-one trade that brought
Von Hayes to Philadelphia was a bad move. No one
can deny that Hayes had his moments with the
Phillies. One of his finest came on June 11, 1985,
when the Phils were facing the New York Mets.
Hayes homered off Tom Gorman in the first inning.
Little did he know he was just getting started. The
Phillies batted around and later in the first, Hayes
was up again, this time with the bases loaded. He
delivered a grand slam, becoming the first player
in history to hit two home runs in the first inning.
Hayes wasn't the only Phillie to have a big day. They
all did in a 26–7 win over the Mets.

84 Five for One

Von Hayes was a good outfielder—he could hit with
decent power, had great speed, and knew how to
play—but was he worth five players in a trade? That
question hung over Hayes from the moment the
Phillies traded Manny Trillo, George Vukovich, Jay
Baller, Jerry Willard, and Julio Franco to the Cleveland
Indians before the 1983 season. To this day, it remains
one of those events in Phillies history that lives on, a
part of the fabric of the franchise.

Von Hayes

William Penn's statue atop City Hall
Inset: Mickey Morandini

85 The Curse of Billy Penn

For years, there was an understanding in Philadelphia that no building would be taller than the statue of city founder William Penn, which stands atop City Hall. Then the first building at nearby Liberty Place opened in March 1987, topping out nearly 400 feet higher than Penn's statue. After that, none of Philadelphia's professional teams—the Phillies, the Eagles, the Flyers, or the Sixers—won a championship. Until 2008.

86 Three for One

Phillies second baseman Mickey Morandini pulled off one of baseball's rarest feats on September 20, 1992, against the Pittsburgh Pirates. In the sixth inning, Morandini made an unassisted triple play, one of only six in National League history. He did it by spearing a line drive off the bat of Jeff King, stepping on second to double up Andy Van Slyke, then tagging the runner who had left first base— a guy by the name of Barry Bonds.

"IT MAKES A FAN WONDER HOW LONG THEY'LL BE UNDER, THE CURSE OF BILLY PENN."

—Ryan Parker, lyrics from "The Curse of Billy Penn"

87 John Kruk

When Kruk arrived in Philadelphia in June 1989, after being traded from the San Diego Padres, few could have imagined the lasting impact he would have on the Phillies and the game. Kruk was a good player—a three-time All-Star in Philadelphia—but he became more than that. With a knack for hitting, a beefy physique, and a sense of humor, Kruk turned into a local hero. It was Kruk who famously said, "Lady, I'm not an athlete. I'm a baseball player." He was a better athlete than he let on, and his personality led to a successful television career after he finished playing.

88 Kruk Versus Johnson

Who says baseball can't be funny? When Kruk stepped into the batter's box to face Seattle's Randy Johnson in the 1993 All-Star Game, it became more than an at bat. It was, well, something different. The 6-foot, 10-inch Johnson whizzed a 98-mile-per-hour fastball over Kruk's head on the first pitch, prompting a crazy swing from the Phillies first baseman, and everything went sideways from there. Kruk, who acted like Fred Sanford feigning a heart attack, gingerly stepped back into the batter's box, but only so far. Facing Johnson, Kruk may have been closer to the on-deck circle than home plate. It became a classic moment in All-Star history, even if it wasn't classic baseball.

"IT'S AMAZING THAT
FANS WANT TO SEE
ME PLAY. IT'S KIND
OF SCARY. I GUESS
THAT'S WHAT IS
WRONG WITH
OUR SOCIETY."

—John Kruk

89 Nails

Lenny Dykstra was the personification of toughness during his days in Philadelphia, where he was an integral part of the 1993 National League championship squad. Dykstra, who played outfield and was a pesky leadoff hitter, had an uncommon fire. With his cheek stuffed with tobacco, Dykstra's nickname, "Nails," fit him perfectly. He was a three-time All-Star with the Phillies, despite the injuries that limited him: He was hurt in an auto accident and later broke his collarbone crashing into the outfield wall in Cincinnati in 1991. During the 1993 season, however, Dykstra was an unstoppable force. He set a major-league record with 773 plate appearances and seemed to provide the Phillies with whatever they needed, including four home runs in the World Series against Toronto. After baseball, Dykstra became an influential figure in the investment world, offering business advice to other ballplayers and writing an investment strategy column for TheStreet.com.

90 The Never-Ending Doubleheader

On July 2, 1993, the Phillies and San Diego began a doubleheader in Veterans Stadium, never imagining it wouldn't conclude until shortly before sunrise the next day. For the record, the teams split the two games, with San Diego winning the first, 5–2, and the Phillies taking the nightcap, 6–5 in 10 innings. But it was unlike any other doubleheader. The first game took 8 hours, 28 minutes to complete because of three rain delays that totaled nearly six hours. During the delays, there was discussion of postponing the second game for a day, but the umpires decided to keep playing. That meant the second game didn't start until 1:28 a.m. It was 4:40 a.m. when it ended—the latest finish ever—and only about 1,000 of the original 54,617 fans in attendance remained.

Lenny Dykstra

Coach Larry Bowa and Lenny Dykstra celebrate Dykstra's game-winning, tenth-inning home run in Game 5 of the 1993 NLCS.

91 1993

One year after finishing last, the Phillies owned the National League East in 1993 and rolled into the World Series, which they would lose to the Toronto Blue Jays. It was the only winning season the Phillies had in the 1990s, but it was full of moments and memories. It began with the Phillies building a 45–17 record, leading the division for all but one day of the season. With a tough, scruffy group led by John Kruk, Lenny Dykstra, Mitch Williams, and Curt Schilling, the Phillies went 97–65, then bumped off the favored Braves in the National League playoffs. Manager Jim Fregosi's squad came from behind, down 2 games to 1, to win the last three games against the Braves in the playoffs, but it couldn't duplicate the magic in the Series, especially after losing a tough 15–14 decision in Game 4 against the Blue Jays. Joe Carter's walk-off, Series-ending three-run homer in Game 6 ended the Phillies' season, but the thrill lives on.

92 Curt Schilling

For many of his nine seasons with the Phillies, Schilling was the ace of the pitching staff, laying the foundation of an outstanding career. During the Phillies' pennant-winning season in 1993, Schilling began to build his reputation as an exceptional postseason pitcher. With power and confidence, Schilling played a huge role in Philadelphia's success. He was named the Most Valuable Player of the 1993 NLCS, though he never got a victory in the series against Atlanta. Schilling pitched brilliantly, however, with a 1.69 earned run average and 19 strikeouts against a team that had won 104 regular-season games. In the World Series, Schilling came up with a critical five-hit shutout victory over Toronto in Game 5 to keep the Phillies' hopes alive. He has remained a significant figure in the game after his days in Philadelphia, and his blog, 38pitches.com, allows fans to keep up with Schilling and his thoughts on the game.

93 Wild Thing

The Phillies knew what they were getting when they acquired Mitch "Wild Thing" Williams from the Cubs in 1991—a left-handed relief pitcher with a ferocious fastball and occasional control issues. Wild Thing became a fan favorite in his early days with the Phillies, but ultimately he would be remembered for allowing Philadelphia hearts to be broken again. During the 1993 World Series against Toronto, Williams was responsible for allowing the Blue Jays to rally for a 15–14 victory in Game 4, putting the Jays up 3 games to 1 and creating a firestorm among Phillies fans. It would only get worse. In Game 6, after the Phillies scored five late runs to take a 6–5 lead, fueling the dream of getting to Game 7, it was Williams' 2–2 pitch that Joe Carter clobbered over the left-field wall for a three-run, Series-winning home run that ensured Wild Thing's days in Philadelphia were over.

Curt Schilling and
Darren Daulton,
1993 World Series

94 The Retired Numbers

1: Richie Ashburn
14: Jim Bunning
20: Mike Schmidt
32: Steve Carlton
36: Robin Roberts
P: Grover Cleveland Alexander
P (Old English): Chuck Klein

95 John Vukovich

For a man whose career batting average was .161 while playing parts of 10 major-league seasons (seven with the Phillies), John Vukovich's impact was enormous. By the time he died at age 59, Vukovich had spent 41 years in professional baseball, and he was a part of the Phillies organization for 31 of those seasons. Vukovich was the longest-tenured coach in Phillies history, teaching the game in his old-school style for 17 consecutive seasons and working for six different managers. When he passed away in 2007, the Phillies remembered him by wearing a black patch on their uniforms during the season.

"JOHN VUKOVICH WAS THE EPITOME OF THE PHRASE 'A BASEBALL MAN.'"

—Harry Kalas

96 Citizens Bank Park

The Phillies' new home, which opened in 2004, is among the finest ballparks in the country, offering a view of the Philadelphia skyline and all the comforts of modern-day parks. Seating 43,500, Citizens Bank Park celebrates the city and the franchise. There is a Wall of Fame in center field and a multitude of options for hungry fans. Of course there are hoagies and cheesesteaks. There's also Bull's BBQ, run by former Phillie Greg Luzinski; Harry the K's bar; and Ashburn Alley. There's even a Build-A-Bear workshop at the stadium, where fans can make their own little Phillie Phanatic to take home as a souvenir.

Opening day, 2007

97 Jimmy Rollins

J-Roll is part of the new generation of Phillies stars, playing shortstop and providing the emotional heartbeat of the team. He has never been shy about speaking his mind, proclaiming prior to the 2007 season that the Phillies were the team to beat in the National League. With a rare blend of speed and power, Rollins was named the 2007 National League MVP after becoming only the fourth player in history to have at least 20 home runs, 20 doubles, 20 triples, and 20 stolen bases in the same season. Rollins also put together a 38-game hitting streak that started at the end of the 2005 season and continued into 2006.

"JIMMY ROLLINS IS WHAT MAKES OUR OFFENSE GO. JIMMY IS WHAT I LIKE TO CALL OUR CATALYST."

—Charlie Manuel

98 Ryan Howard

In terms of pure power, they don't come much more powerful than the Phillies' first baseman, who seems intent on rewriting some home-run records. Howard quickly established himself as one of the game's most prodigious sluggers in 2005, winning the National League Rookie of the Year award. One year later, he was named the National League MVP after becoming the eighth player in history to hit 58 home runs in a season. In 2007, Howard added another 47 home runs and 136 RBI, placing second in the league in both categories.

In 2008, Howard put himself in an elite group when he became the first player in 47 seasons to lead the league in home runs and RBI while also winning the World Series. The only other players to have that distinction are Babe Ruth, Hank Greenberg, Mickey Mantle, Hank Aaron, and Roger Maris.

99 Chase Utley

At second base, Utley is part of the Phillies' loaded infield with first baseman Ryan Howard and shortstop Jimmy Rollins, giving the team one of the most dynamic sets of young players in the game. Utley has a classic style about him, and he announced his arrival in style, hitting a grand slam in his first major-league start. He has become a fixture at second base for the Phillies as well as one of the team's most popular players in recent years. In four consecutive seasons, starting in 2005, Utley has homered at least 22 times and driven in more than 100 runs each year.

"I JUST WANT TO GET BETTER. I WANT TO KEEP IMPROVING."

—Chase Utley

Chase Utley tags out the Mets' Moises Alou.

100 The Comeback

It didn't quite make up for the collapse of 1964, but it came close. In mid-September 2007, the Phillies were seven games behind the New York Mets in the NL East and, in most minds, out of the race. But a funny thing happened along the way—the Mets went stone cold and the Phillies got red hot. It took just 16 days for the Phillies to replace the Mets in first place, but the division wasn't decided until the final day of the regular season, which began with the teams tied for first. The Mets' day came apart early, and the Phillies clinched the division with a victory over the Washington Nationals, with 44-year-old Jamie Moyer pitching the decisive game. The Phillies were later swept in three games by the Colorado Rockies in the divisional playoffs, but it was just a prelude to an unforgettable 2008 season.

"THE BIGGEST GAME OF THE YEAR, AND WE HAVE TO WIN."

—Chase Utley on the last game of the 2007 regular season

101 Faith

With just one World Series championship through more than a century of baseball, getting the second one couldn't be easy for the Phillies. It required enduring rain, wind, cold, mud, the Tampa Bay Rays, and one game that spanned three days. It meant getting to the edge, close enough to put the champagne on ice, then having to wait and wonder if it was all a cruel hoax, if somehow what seemed so close would slip away again. You don't lose more than 10,000 games without having your faith tested. But the 2008 Phillies passed every test. They did it with Cole Hamels turning into Sandy Koufax. They did it with Shane Victorino getting key hits, Brad Lidge shutting down every late-inning challenge, and Charlie Manuel making all the right moves. They did it with so many others—Ryan Howard, Jimmy Rollins, Chase Utley, Jayson Werth, and a legion of fans who had waited 28 long seasons for another World Series championship. It was, after all, a matter of faith.

Shane Victorino leaps onto the pile of teammates celebrating the 2008 World Series title.

Chris Coste signs autographs at spring training.

Acknowledgments

A special thank you goes out to Ann Stratton, Jennifer Levesque, and the many good people at Stewart, Tabori & Chang, where they believe in the value and art of good books. Also, a special thanks to copy editor Richard Slovak, who is a writer's best friend, correcting the mistakes and offering suggestions to improve the project.

And to the folks who provide the wonderful photographs you see in these books: Ted Ciuzio at AP Images, Pat Kelly at the National Baseball Hall of Fame Library, and everyone in the New York Public Library Photographic Services department. Your contributions are what make these books so special.

There are more than 101 reasons to love Mary Tiegreen, whose vision led to the creation of this book and many others like it. And as always, a word of thanks to my brother, Dave, who brought it all together and makes it seem easy.

To my brother-in-law John, my sister Edie, and the entire McGlone clan where the Phillies are considered a part of the family, a special thanks for sharing not only the details of the Phillies history but also the emotional investment that comes with being a fan.

To my wife, Tamera, and my daughter, Molly; my parents, Ron and Beth Green; the Greens of New York as well as the Macchias and Brad Caplanides, thank you for everything.

And, finally, to the Phillies, who haven't always won championships but have won a ton of hearts, thanks for giving us these stories to tell.

A Tiegreen Book

Published in 2009 by Stewart, Tabori & Chang
An imprint of Harry N. Abrams, Inc.

All rights reserved. No portion of this book may be reproduced, stored in a retrieval system, or transmitted in any form or by any means, mechanical, electronic, photocopying, recording, or otherwise, without written permission from the publisher.

Stewart, Tabori & Chang books are available at special discounts when purchased in quantity for premiums and promotions as well as fundraising or educational use. Special editions can also be created to specification. For details, contact specialmarkets@hnabooks.com.

Library of Congress Cataloging-in-Publication Data:

Green, Ron, 1956-
   101 reasons to love the Phillies /
   by Ron Green, Jr.
     p. cm.
   ISBN 978-1-58479-755-5
1. Philadelphia Phillies (Baseball team)—Miscellanea. I. Title.
   II. Title: One hundred one reasons to love the Phillies.
   III. Title: One hundred and one reasons to love the Phillies.
GV875.P45G74 2009
796.357'640974811—dc22
2008038814

Text copyright © 2009 Ron Green, Jr.
Compilation copyright © 2009 Mary Tiegreen

Editor: Ann Stratton
Designer: David Green, Brightgreen Design
Production Manager: Tina Cameron

101 Reasons to Love the Phillies is a book in the 101 REASONS TO LOVE™ series.

101 REASONS TO LOVE™ is a trademark of Mary Tiegreen and Hubert Pedroli.

Printed and bound in China
10 9 8 7 6 5 4 3 2

HNA ▌▌▌▌▌
harry n. abrams, inc.
a subsidiary of La Martinière Groupe

115 West 18th Street
New York, NY 10011
www.hnabooks.com

Photo Credits

Pages 1, 2–3, 6–7, 32, 34–35, 36–37, 38, 40, 42 (portrait), 43, 45, 46–47, 48, 50 (portrait), 51, 52, 54–55, 56, 58, 61, 63, 64, 67, 68–69, 70, 72, 75, 77, 79, 80, 82 (inset), 83, 84, 85 (portrait), 86–87, 88, 91, 93, 94, 95 (inset), 97, 99, 100, 103, 104, 106–107, 108–109, 110–111, 112–113, 114–115, 116–117, and 118 courtesy of AP Images.

Pages 5 (ball), 60 (inset), and 73 (ball) courtesy of John McGlone.

Pages 8–9 and 12 courtesy of the New York Public Library A.G. Spalding Baseball Collection.

Pages 10–11, 14 (card), 15 (card), 16–17, 20, 24–25, 26, and 29 courtesy of the Library of Congress Prints and Photographs department.

Pages 18, 22, and 31 courtesy of the National Baseball Hall of Fame Library.

Pages 49 (card), 53 (card), 59 (card), 62 (card), 76 (ball), and 120 (card) courtesy of David Green, Brightgreen Design.

MANAGER
GENE MAUCH